The Week That Changed the World

Daily Reflections for Holy Week

STEVEN D. BROOKS

WESTBOW
PRESS®

A DIVISION OF THOMAS NELSON
& ZONDERVAN

WestBow Press books may be ordered through booksellers or by contacting:

WestBow Press
A Division of Thomas Nelson & Zondervan
1663 Liberty Drive
Bloomington, IN 47403
www.westbowpress.com
844-714-3454

Scripture quotations are from The ESV® Bible (The Holy Bible, English Standard Version®), copyright © 2001 by Crossway, a publishing ministry of Good News Publishers. Used by permission. All rights reserved.

ISBN: 978-1-6642-2182-6 (sc)
ISBN: 978-1-6642-2184-0 (hc)
ISBN: 978-1-6642-2183-3 (e)

Library of Congress Control Number: 2021901930

Print information available on the last page.

WestBow Press rev. date: 02/11/2021

No pain, no palm;

no thorns, no throne;

no gall, no glory;

no cross, no crown.

William Penn (1644–1718)

Be sure to check out Worship Quest Ministries

Encouraging worship renewal and spiritual
formation for the global Christian church

worshipquest.net

Contents

Introduction

[By this gospel you are saved] . . . For I delivered to you as of first importance what I also received: that Christ died for our sins in accordance with the Scriptures, that he was buried, that he was raised on the third day in accordance with the Scriptures.

1 Corinthians 15:2–4

The Christian church follows a pattern of time different than that of the world. Within corporate gatherings, the church focuses their worship upon the Christ–event— birth, life, death, resurrection, ascension, and promised return of the Savior; while remembering the fullness of God's story of creation—God created all things seen and unseen to share in his community; incarnation— God sent Jesus to earth to redeem the fallen creation accomplishing for us what we could not accomplish for ourselves; and re–creation—the finale of the story when Jesus returns at the end of the age to restore his world and make all things new again. This pattern of sacred time was developed into a calendar as a means to remember all that Christ had done for the world. Within that traditional church calendar, there is a season where followers of Christ are invited to journey toward Easter by looking within to identify the ways in which we as individuals, the church, and society fall short of God's vision for us. This season of Lent is a time set aside for letting God work within us as we engage in the process of self–examination; casting off those habits and practices which lead us away from focusing on God, while taking on that which contributes to our spiritual vitality, restoration, and renewal. This season intensifies our echo of the psalmist's request for God to search and cleanse us of all sin and lead us on the right path.

> Search me, O God, and know my heart!
> Try me and know my thoughts! And see if
> there be any grievous way in me, and lead
> me in the way everlasting! (Ps 139:23–24)

The word "Lent" comes from the Old English word *lencten*, which has commonly been interpreted to mean "spring," named so for the time of the year in which it occurs. The literal interpretation of the term is "lengthen," referring to the days beginning to get longer, which occurs in the spring season.

Spring is a season for renewal. The new year has come and gone. Winter has passed and it is time to transition into a season of rejuvenation and cleansing. It is a time for "spring cleaning". The phrase "spring cleaning" may be a familiar term. Some suggest that the origins of spring cleaning date back to the ancient Jewish practice of thoroughly cleansing the home in anticipation of the springtime festival of Passover (Pesach), when the Jewish community remembers their deliverance out of

Egypt following their captivity. Another idea emerges from times when winter left homes coated with a layer of soot and grime due to burning wood and coal to heat the home. Proper cleaning required opening windows to let the soot out, which, of course, could only be done during warmer weather, which started in spring. Although many people today don't warm their homes in the winter months with coal burning devices, the idea of spring cleaning has remained an important part of many cultures as each year people sense the proclivity to look around their homes and purge non–essential items. Nearly everyone goes through a cycle of cleaning out the clutter in homes, bedrooms, or dorm rooms. It is a time of cleansing and renewal.

In the same way, this is also what Lent is about. It is a "spring cleaning" for our souls. We search within to find all that really doesn't need to be there, or shouldn't be there, and we empty those things from our lives, inviting Christ to fill their place. In this way, Lent is as much about taking on as it is about giving up. During this season, we are encouraged to practice ***engaging spiritual habits***—such as prayer, service, and meditation; as well as ***abstaining spiritual habits***—such as fasting, silence, and solitude. Lent is meant to be a time of spiritual renewal in which we take stock of our relationship with God and our neighbor, seek God's forgiveness for the sins we have committed, and strive to make positive changes in our daily living.

Spring is also the season of new beginnings. Just as winter symbolizes death, spring symbolizes new life. Trees, plants, flowers, and fields begin to turn green as new life starts to emerge. Likewise Christianity provides new life and we are reminded of this especially during Easter. In the Christian faith, we are assured that not only did Jesus rise from the dead, but every follower of Christ also gains new life when they place their faith in Jesus.

> Therefore, if anyone is in Christ, he is a new creation. The old has passed away; behold, the new has come. (2 Cor 5:17)

The believer's new life, their new creation, springs from Jesus Christ. Just as nature can't be held back in the spring from re–emerging from the dreary and confining winter, the earth could not hold Christ as he conquered death and emerged victorious up from the grave. Jesus's triumph over death gives anyone who believes in him a joyful hope for a new life and a restored relationship with God.

Lent is a season of preparation intended to prepare the follower of Christ for the celebration of new life and new beginnings through resurrection. Lent is a time to ask God to cleanse us within and a time to prepare for a season of new beginnings by reflecting upon death and mortality—"For he knows how we are formed; he remembers that we are dust" (Ps 103:14)—and looking ahead to new life in Christ—"We were buried therefore with him by baptism into death, in order that, just as Christ was raised from the dead by the glory of the Father, we too might walk in newness of life" (Rom 6:4). During the season of Lent we anticipate the revitalization of an Easter season dedicated to renewal, new beginnings, re–birth, and new life.

Lent is not the only time for self–examination, yet the Christian Year calendar offers the Christ follower designated opportunities to engage in focused spiritual development. Practically speaking, on the anniversary of my wedding, I go to extra effort to express my love for my wife. I might take her out for a nice dinner at a fancy restaurant, send her a bouquet of extravagant red roses, and am generous with how often I say, "I love you". Now since I did all of this on our anniversary, I don't have to take her out for dinner, buy her flowers, or say, "I love you" the rest of the year, right? Of course not! I continue to do those things throughout the year to express my love for her and my gratitude to God for allowing me to be her husband. The restaurants may not be as fancy, the flowers may not be red roses, but it is important to continue expressing my love for her on a regular basis. Yet on our anniversary, the intensity of the expression increases because it is a special time. Similarly, although the spiritual emphases of Lent—searching within asking God to cleanse us and renew us—should be a regular daily occurrence in our lives, the season of Lent gives us a designated time in the calendar to focus our attention on being spiritually cleansed and renewed in Christ Jesus.

During the last week of the season of Lent, called Holy Week, we join Jesus as he walked through the final stretch toward his death and resurrection. The first Holy Week began with Jesus riding into Jerusalem being praised as king and culminated in Jesus's earthly body lying in a tomb. This astonishing week of contrast encompasses such a sweeping range of emotion and expression for the believer—from unrestrained praise to deep mourning. This is a thought provoking week. This is a heart–wrenching week. It is a week that leads to the most important event in history—the resurrection of Jesus, our Redeemer and King. It is truly a week that changed the world.

This collection of daily reflections follows the footsteps of Jesus as he walked through the last week of his earthly life. Theologians have considered the chronological order of the events of this week, with slight differences of opinion on which days certain events occurred. I will follow the most widely accepted order for the steps that Jesus took between the triumphal entrance into Jerusalem and his burial in Joseph of Arimathea's tomb.

The entire life of Jesus was a prelude to the events and teachings during his final week. All that Jesus did during his life led to this moment. One half of all four Gospel accounts focus on the final week of Jesus's ministry. If this week was so important to the Gospel writers, should we not consider its importance for our own lives today? By reflecting upon the events of Holy Week, we gain a greater understanding of the mission of Jesus.

Certain days within Holy Week have specific names, while others simply include the prefix "holy" to signify that it is the individual day that falls during Holy Week.

Here is a brief preview of what is to come:

Palm/Passion Sunday—Jesus entered Jerusalem accompanied by the praise of the crowd.

Holy Monday—Jesus cleared the temple.

Holy Tuesday—Jesus's authority was questioned.

Holy Wednesday—Jesus continued to teach in the temple and Judas agreed to betray Jesus.

Maundy Thursday—Jesus celebrated Passover with his disciples.

Good Friday—Jesus was put to death.

Holy Saturday—The body of Jesus laid in the grave; and the disciples hid in fear.

Easter Sunday—The beginning of the Easter season—Christ has risen!

Follow along with me. Let's journey together as Jesus leads us from praise to mourning and from death to new life.

One word of encouragement before we go further— if you have not been practicing spiritual disciplines of abstinence and engagement throughout the entire season of Lent, I encourage you to do so during this final week of the season. Between Palm/Passion Sunday and Holy Saturday, select something you will abstain from (fasting, solitude, etc.) and choose to engage in a spiritual habit that will encourage more of Jesus in its place (Bible reading, prayer, etc.). For instance, consider replacing eating sweets with doing this devotional each day. I firmly believe that practicing spiritual disciplines of abstinence and engagement will make a significant impact upon your spiritual life.

How To Read This Book

The first Holy Week was a week that changed the world, but sometimes we're so busy we don't consider how it's supposed to change us. This book is intended to help you see how God's word can make an impact in your life during this significant time of year. These reflections will help you walk meaningfully through Holy Week. We want to take the ancient journey with Jesus and yet bring it into our world realizing that this week changes everything, including today. So how do you get the most out of this book?

Quiet Yourself. Find a quiet place where you are not easily distracted. Plan to spend anywhere from 15–30 minutes (the more time the better, but even a small amount of time is better than no time at all).

Pray. Even before you open this book or your Bible, spend some time worshiping God through prayer. If you're having a hard time figuring out what to say, open your Bible to the Psalms and read a few verses as a prayer to God. After that, confess any sin you may have in your life (1 John 1:9) and ask God to reveal what he wants to show you through the daily reflection.

Read. Next, read the Bible passage listed in the day's reflection as well as the reflection itself. As you read, be aware of the context of the passage. When you are done reading, consider what the scripture passage and daily reflection are about, what God is revealing to you, and how God would like you to respond.

Apply. Continue pondering what God has done in history on your behalf and let it make an impact upon your life today as you consider the "Holy Week Today" section.

Worship. Finally, close your time in worship utilizing the prayer and hymn text provided.

Palm/Passion Sunday

Hosanna! Lord, Save Us!

Read: Luke 19:28–44

Many know the Sunday before Easter as Palm Sunday. Others refer to it as Passion Sunday. The difference in titles encourages us to focus on the distinct aspects of the events of this day. It is as though this day's events fall on two sides of a coin.

On one side of the coin, we remember and celebrate when Jesus rode into Jerusalem on a donkey fulfilling the prophecy of Zechariah.

> Behold, your king is coming to you;
> righteous and having salvation is he,
> humble and mounted on a donkey, on a
> colt, the foal of a donkey. (Zech 9:9)

As we read in the Gospels, Jesus traveled to Jerusalem along with crowds of other Jews to celebrate the Passover. This tradition of the Jewish people had been around since the time of Moses (as prescribed in Exodus and Deuteronomy). According to the Gospel of John, Jesus and many of his followers journeyed the two miles from Bethany on that Sunday, arriving just outside of Jerusalem. This journey down the hill from Bethany, through the Mount of Olives and Gethsemane, into the Kidron Valley, and up the hill into Jerusalem would have been clearly visible by those in Jerusalem. As was the custom, pilgrims that had already arrived in the city went out to greet newly arriving groups. There were some who had undoubtedly come into contact with Jesus at some point. Others had never seen Jesus but had probably heard about him because of the miracles he performed and they were caught up in the excitement. As a result, a sizeable crowd of people gathered to welcome Jesus.

> The next day the large crowd that had come to the feast heard that Jesus was coming to Jerusalem. So they took branches of palm trees and went out to meet him. (John 12:12–13)

Some laid their cloaks down in front of Jesus. Others grabbed palm branches and began waving them (a Jewish national symbol conveying the notion of victory over one's enemies). Their actions were accompanied by loud shouts of praise directed toward Jesus, hailing him as king.

Hosanna to the Son of David! Blessed is
he who comes in the name of the Lord!
Hosanna in the highest! (Matt 21:9)

Their exclamations echoed the words of the psalmist:

Save us, we pray, O Lord! O Lord, we pray,
give us success! Blessed is he who comes in
the name of the Lord! We bless you from
the house of the Lord. (Ps 118:25–26)

Previously, Jesus had intentionally avoided public acclamation, most often even fled from it, but this time, upon entering Jerusalem, he accepts the praise of the people. Yet even in this moment Jesus responds in a way that is different than the people expected. He doesn't present himself as a rival to Caesar; he doesn't claim to be a political messiah or the warrior king the multitude had hoped for. Instead of entering Jerusalem on a majestic horse or chariot, he enters on a donkey, a sign of peace—and not just any donkey, but one on which no one had ever sat (Mark 11:2), which is the prerogative of a king.

There is no doubt—this was a time of great

celebration! Shouts of praise, symbols of victory, and a kingly, albeit unconventional, entrance. The celebration was magnificent, but we must not stop at the waving of palms. We must read farther on. In his Gospel, Luke shares the event immediately after Jesus's entrance to Jerusalem. As the people raised their voices, the Pharisees became upset and demanded that Jesus silence the crowd. Jesus responded that he would not quiet the crowd because if he did, the rocks would cry out in praise (Luke 19:39–40). It is what happens next that should cause us to pause and reflect. It is the "passion" side of the coin of this day. Following the shouts of praise, as Jesus looked over the city of Jerusalem, he wept.

> And when he drew near and saw the city,
> he wept over it. (Luke 19:41)

This was not a good cry. This was a grieving cry, for Jesus understood the path that was set before him—a path that began with this entrance. Jesus knew that by the end of the week the shouts of praise that were ringing in his ears would turn to malicious cries for his death. He saw the sin in the people's hearts and their own refusal to allow him to cleanse them. He knew that their shouts of "hosanna," meaning "save us" were words that they fully did not comprehend. They didn't really understand what they were asking, at least not in the sense that really mattered—spiritually. In fact, unbeknownst to them, their cries of "hosanna" were directing Jesus to the dreadful moment and place where he could actually fulfill their appeal to save them—the cross. And so Jesus wept. Each step he took from that point forward took him one step closer to the cross.

French clergyman Bernard of Clairvaux (1090–1153), in his "Sermons for Lent and the Easter Season," offered some thoughts about Christ's entry into Jerusalem and its contrast with the day of his crucifixion:

> How different the cries, "Away with him, away with him, crucify him," and then, "Blessed is he who comes in the name of the Lord, hosanna, in the highest!" How different the cries are that now are calling him "King of Israel" and then in a few days' time will be saying, "We have no king but Caesar!" What a contrast between the green branches and the cross, between the flowers and the thorns! Before they

were offering their own clothes for him to walk upon, and so soon afterwards they are stripping him of his, and casting lots upon them.

In his Gospel account Matthew informs us that Jesus felt compelled to go to Jerusalem to accomplish his mission.

> From that time Jesus began to show his disciples that he must go to Jerusalem and suffer many things from the elders and chief priests and scribes, and be killed, and on the third day be raised. (Matt 16:21)

This was the work Jesus had been sent to do. He had come to save the lost.

> For the Son of Man came to seek and to save the lost. (Luke 19:10)

Palm Sunday was the "beginning of the end" of Jesus's earthly work. As Jesus entered Jerusalem, he neared the culmination of a long journey toward the cross. Now was the time, beginning in this place, to secure that salvation. It is within the events of this day that we see the "passion" (suffering) and the "palm" (praise). This was, and is, the journey of Holy Week.

Holy Week Today

What impact should this have on our lives today? The story of the triumphal entry is one of contrasts. On that day there were two groups of people—those praising and those complaining. In which group would you have been on that first Palm Sunday—among the disciples who welcomed him with praise or among the skeptics and critics? It's easy to condemn those who condemned Jesus, but would we have acted any differently?

May you welcome him into your life during this Holy Week. Pray the following prayer as a way of confirming your openness to God doing an incredible work in your life.

Palm/Passion Sunday Prayer

Hosanna.

Lord, save us.

Lord Jesus, save us, your children.

Lord Jesus Christ, save us, your children, from our sin.

Lord Jesus, forgive us our sin and help us to reject future sin and the power it may have over us.

Lord Jesus, save us, your children, from sin.

Lord Jesus, save us, your children.

Lord, save us.

Hosanna.

Hosanna, Loud Hosanna

Hosanna, loud hosanna,
the little children sang:
Through pillared court and temple
the lovely anthem rang.
To Jesus, who had blessed them
close folded to his breast,
the children sang their praises,
the simplest and the best.

From Olivet they followed
mid an exultant crowd,
the victor palm branch waving,
and chanting clear and loud.
The Lord of men and angels
rode on in lowly state,
nor scorned that little children
should on his bidding wait.

"Hosanna in the highest!"
that ancient song we sing,
for Christ is our Redeemer,
the Lord of heaven our King.

STEVEN D. BROOKS

O may we ever praise him
with heart and life and voice,
and in his blissful presence
eternally rejoice!

Jeannette Threlfall (1873)

Holy Monday

A Time for Cleansing

Read: Mark 11:12–19

Yesterday was a fulfilling and exciting day for Jesus and his disciples. It was a day filled with exuberant praise directed toward Jesus. Jesus was finally receiving the praise he was due. Or was he? You see, the people were praising the king they thought he was. The king they wanted and expected him to be. Not the King he actually was—and is.

This veil of darkness over the people's understanding of who Jesus was and what he had come to accomplish caused a deep sadness within Jesus. As a result, he wept over the city.

> And when he drew near and saw the city, he wept over it, saying, "Would that you, even you, had known on this day the things that make for peace! But now they are hidden from your eyes. For the days will come upon you, when your enemies will set up a barricade around you and surround you and hem you in on every side and tear you down to the ground, you and your children within you. And they

will not leave one stone upon another in you, because you did not know the time of your visitation." (Luke 19:41–44)

He wept even as he expressed a willingness to make peace if they would have acknowledged the terms of peace. When Jesus said, "You did not know the time of your visitation," he meant that his coming was the coming of God for their redemption, for their salvation. Jesus came to offer ultimate salvation and to cleanse them spiritually, but their blindness to the reality of the situation prevented them from fully receiving all that Jesus was offering. And so Jesus continued his journey toward the cross.

In the evening of Palm Sunday, Jesus returned to Bethany, the same city where he would be anointed later in the week. Having spent the night in Bethany, Jesus and his disciples returned to Jerusalem on Monday morning. On the walk from Bethany to Jerusalem, they passed by a fig tree full of leaves. Jesus was hungry so he walked over to the tree to grab a bite to eat, but the tree was barren. The fact that the fig tree had leaves meant that there was a good possibility that there would be figs on it as well (as the fruit generally appeared at the same time, if not shortly after the appearance of the leaves). So what did Jesus do? Did he command the tree to blossom, to produce fruit for him to eat? No, he cursed the tree and used it as a teaching opportunity (we will look at that in tomorrow's reflection).

Once Jesus arrived in Jerusalem, he went to the temple. Matthew (21:12–13), Mark (11:15–17), and Luke (19:45–46) tell us that upon his arrival, Jesus cleared the temple of the "money–changers." Here we see Jesus expressing righteous anger as he observed merchants who had turned God's house of prayer into a profit–seeking business. In his anger Jesus turned over tables and drove the merchants away from the temple area. We must understand, Jesus was not upset because people were selling items. The temple and marketplace had been connected for many years. This was the cultural center of the city. Jesus knew and understood this. The reason for this response at this particular time was because the merchants had crept into the temple proper and were taking advantage of the worshipers—especially those who traveled to Jerusalem for the feast of Passover and needed to purchase animals for sacrifice. Instead of traveling long distances with animals, which was rather impractical, Jewish worshipers would simply purchase their sacrifices once they arrived in Jerusalem. However, the merchants were raising their prices knowing the worshipers had no other choice but to buy from them. The merchants had placed profit above worship. When Jesus speaks of the "den of robbers" (Mark 11:17), he is not only referring to the improper location of the trading, but also the dishonesty of the merchants.

Most Jews also paid the temple tax at Passover and money–changers were there to convert Roman coinage into appropriate currency since pagan mottoes on Roman money made it unacceptable for the house of Yahweh. Though not inherently evil, these practices became occasions for sin. Jewish pilgrims paid exorbitant rates to exchange money, and sellers exploited those in poverty, overcharging for the poor man's offering of pigeons and doves (Lev 5:7). To make things worse, these merchants set up shop in the outer Court of the Gentiles, making it useless as a place of prayer due to the hustle and bustle that the buying and selling generated.

Jesus looked around and saw that the marketplace was hindering rather than encouraging many worshipers. As a result, Jesus, jealous for God to receive his rightful worship, overturned tables and forced the money–changers and sellers out of the area.

This action of clearing the temple is especially appropriate in light of yesterday—Palm Sunday. Then, the crowds were shouting his praises while waving palms of victory, but now people are being distracted from worship. Jesus wouldn't let the Pharisee's quiet the crowd on Palm Sunday and he was not going to let the merchants and money–changers hinder the people's worship on this day. This important act showed Jesus as having authority to purify and take charge of the temple, an undertaking fit for the Messiah, according to Ezekiel (43:1–12), and this only put him more at odds with the Sanhedrin.

At the end of this eventful second day of Holy Week, Jesus with his disciples returned to Bethany and rested for the evening (Mark 11:19).

Holy Week Today

When we consider the events of this day in Jesus's life, it is clear that the theme for the day is cleansing. On this day of cleansing, will you join me in searching within to see if there are any areas in our lives that are not bearing fruit? Just like the fig tree and the bustling temple courts during Passover, are you simply putting on a good show while lacking fruitfulness? It's one thing to lack fruit out of season, it's another to lack it while pretending you have it.

Are there any actions or attitudes that are hindering you from worthily worshiping God to the fullest? If so, pray the following prayer asking God to search within and cleanse you from all that actively works to separate you from God.

Holy Monday Prayer

from Psalm 139:23–24

"Search me, O God, and know my heart! Try me and know my thoughts! And see if there be any grievous way in me, and lead me in the way everlasting!"

Cleanse me, Lord, spiritually, emotionally, and physically so that I can be a better ambassador for Christ. Enrich my life with the spiritual nutrients needed so I may bear fruit for you. Help me stay focused on you and not be distracted from worshiping you and you alone.

This is my plea, to you Father, in the name of Jesus, by the power of your Holy Spirit,

Amen.

Come Down, O Love Divine

Come down, O love divine,
seek thou this soul of mine,
and visit it with thine own ardor glowing;
O Comforter, draw near,
within my heart appear,
and kindle it, thy holy flame bestowing.

O let it freely burn,
till earthly passions turn
to dust and ashes in its heat consuming;
And let thy glorious light
shine ever on my sight,
and clothe me round, the while my path illuming.

And so the yearning strong,
with which the soul will long,
shall far outpass the power of human telling;
For none can guess its grace,
till love create a place
wherein the Holy Spirit makes a dwelling.

Bianco da Siena (circa 1434); trans. Richard Frederick
Littledale, Jr. (1867)

Holy Tuesday

By What Authority?

Read: Matthew 21:23–27, 42–46

On Tuesday, Jesus and his disciples returned to Jerusalem from Bethany. During their walk, the disciples saw the fig tree that Jesus cursed the day before. Peter pointed it out and Jesus used it as a teaching opportunity.

> As they passed by in the morning, they saw the fig tree withered away to its roots. And Peter remembered and said to him, "Rabbi, look! The fig tree that you cursed has withered." And Jesus answered them, "Have faith in God. Truly, I say to you, whoever says to this mountain, 'Be taken up and thrown into the sea,' and does not doubt in his heart, but believes that what he says will come to pass, it will be done for him. Therefore I tell you, whatever you ask in prayer, believe that you have received it, and it will be yours. And whenever you stand praying, forgive, if you have anything against anyone, so that your Father also who is in heaven

may forgive you your trespasses." (Mark 11:20–26)

Thus Jesus encouraged the disciples by telling them that with faith, they can do that which seems impossible. We must have faith that God will remove anything that hinders us from bearing fruit for him.

In Matthew's account of this event, he portrays Jesus's words of judgment upon those whose lives are not fully devoted to Christ. Just as the tree was hypocritical— looking one way (fully bloomed), but in reality was something different (barren), so there is judgment for those who are hypocritical in word and deed and for those who should be bearing fruit but do not. Just as the fig tree withered, so God will remove any aspect within us that does not bear fruit.

We must stay focused on Christ, connected to him as branches to a vine, so as to bear fruit and not be led astray.

> Every branch in me that does not bear fruit
> he takes away, and every branch that does
> bear fruit he prunes, that it may bear more
> fruit . . . Abide in me, and I in you. As the

branch cannot bear fruit by itself, unless it abides in the vine, neither can you, unless you abide in me. I am the vine; you are the branches. Whoever abides in me and I in him, he it is that bears much fruit, for apart from me you can do nothing. (John 15:2, 4–5)

Bearing fruit, which Jesus later identified as keeping his commandments (John 15:10), is intimately connected to abiding in him. It is within the scope of abiding in Christ and not apart from it that fruit emerges.

After observing the withered tree and discussing its theological significance, Jesus and his disciples continued toward Jerusalem. When they arrived at the temple, the chief priests and scribes began questioning Jesus's authority—"By what authority are you doing these things, and who gave you this authority?" (Matt 21:23) Faced with their hostility, Jesus refused to answer their questions. Instead, he turned the tables, figuratively this time, and asked them a question—which they could, or would not answer. He then spoke to them in parables, mostly about judgment on the leaders for their refusal to encourage the people to accept God's kingdom invitation and recognize his return at the end of the age. It was also during this discourse that Jesus repeats the "great command" to love God and love others (see Deut 6:5).

What strikes me most about the exchange of questions between Jesus and the religious leaders is the leaders' audacity to question Jesus. Think about this from Jesus's perspective: he knew that in three days he would be beaten and crucified and here are these religious leaders questioning his authority? What an utter waste of time! There had to be more important things to do in order to get ready for Friday . . . and Sunday! And yet Jesus took the time to address them. In a round about way, he told them that his authority is an "out of this world" authority that they could not understand. He responded to their question with a question of his own. Then, when they couldn't answer, Jesus implied that because his authority is greater than any other authority, he would not give them a direct answer to their question. Thus Jesus continued to teach and do what he could to prepare the people for what was to come.

Once more, at the close of day, just as he had done before, Jesus returned to Bethany. He was one day closer to fulfilling the critical act as our Redeemer.

Holy Week Today

The Christian faith is founded on truth. As a result, it will be offensive to many people. Nevertheless we must strive to interact with people within the influence of God's authority filled with true humility. When Jesus was accusatorily questioned, he responded with divine authority, through humility and dignity. He was neither fearful nor timid but always spoke truth. May we seek to do likewise, never compromising the truth for the sake of trying to appear humble or inclusive. If you know the truth, stand for it, regardless of the outcome. Even if it ends relationships. Even if it costs your life.

Is there a situation where you need to speak the truth in love? How can you encourage someone today by your words and actions? In what other ways do you need to be obedient to Jesus?

Holy Tuesday Prayer

Dear Lord, as we continue the journey through Holy Week, help me to trust you more fully, God, and live in your forgiveness, healing, and wholeness. May my heart be renewed. Take away that which is within me that does not bring you glory so I may abide in you and bear fruit in your name.

Give me a heart for those around me to share the gospel of Jesus, full of truth and love.

Father, I pray all of these things, in the authoritative name of Jesus, and the power of the Holy Spirit,

Amen.

Abide With Me

Abide with me: fast falls the eventide;
The darkness deepens; Lord, with me abide.
When other helpers fail and comforts flee,
help of the helpless, O abide with me.

Swift to its close ebbs out life's little day;
Earth's joys grow dim, its glories pass away.
Change and decay in all around I see.
O thou who changest not, abide with me.

I need thy presence every passing hour.
What but thy grace can foil the tempter's power?
Who like thyself my guide and strength can be?
Through cloud and sunshine, O abide with me.

I fear no foe with thee at hand to bless,
ills have no weight, and tears no bitterness.
Where is death's sting? Where, grave, thy victory?
I triumph still, if thou abide with me.

STEVEN D. BROOKS

Hold thou thy cross before my closing eyes.

Shine through the gloom and point me to the skies.

Heaven's morning breaks and earth's vain shadows flee;

In life, in death, O Lord, abide with me.

Henry Francis Lyte (1847); William Henry Monk (1861)

Holy Wednesday

An (Un)Expected Betrayal

Read: Mark 14:1–2, 10–11, 17–21

On Wednesday, the third day after his triumphal entry into the city on Mount Zion, Jesus taught in the temple in Jerusalem. This day's teaching may be summed up in his words recorded by Luke:

> Stay awake at all times, praying that you may have strength to escape all these things that are going to take place, and to stand before the Son of Man. (Luke 21:36)

Even today Jesus desires that we escape the judgment he warned about in his teaching; to stand before God and hear the words, "well done" (Luke 19:17).

When Jesus had finished his teaching, he turned his attention to the disciples and predicted his arrest and crucifixion. The plot against Jesus had begun as the chief priests gathered together in the private residence of Caiaphas to scheme against Jesus. Their verdict against Jesus had already been decided. The only issue was how to get rid of him. Enter Judas:

> Then one of the twelve, whose name was Judas Iscariot, went to the chief priests and

said, "What will you give me if I deliver him over to you?" And they paid him thirty pieces of silver. And from that moment he sought an opportunity to betray him. (Matt 26:14–16)

A devious plot had been set in motion. Judas simply needed to wait for the right time and place for the betrayal.

The account of Judas is an absolute tragic story chronicling at its climax a conspiracy between Judas and Satan. Scripture tells us that when Judas decided to betray Jesus, Satan entered him and the conspiracy was set into motion.

Jesus was troubled in his spirit, and testified, "Truly, truly, I say to you, one of you will betray me." The disciples looked at one another, uncertain of whom he spoke. One of his disciples, whom Jesus loved, was reclining at table at Jesus's side, so Simon Peter motioned to him to ask Jesus of whom he was speaking. So that disciple, leaning back against Jesus, said to him, "Lord, who is it?" Jesus answered, "It is he to whom I will give this morsel of bread when I have dipped it." So when he had dipped the morsel, he gave it to Judas, the son of Simon Iscariot. Then after he had taken the morsel, Satan entered into him. Jesus said to him, "What you are going to do, do quickly." (John 13:21–27)

The chief priests and the scribes were seeking how to put him to death, for they feared the people. Then Satan entered into Judas called Iscariot, who was of the number of the twelve. He went away and conferred with the chief priests and officers how he might betray him to them. (Luke 22:2–4)

This entire situation seems shocking and unexpected, but Jesus wasn't surprised by the events nor the way in which they unfolded. When Jesus referenced Psalm 41:9, "Even my close friend in whom I trusted, who ate my bread, has lifted his heel against me," it is interesting that he omitted the words "whom I trusted" (John

13:18). The most likely reason being, he "knew from the beginning who those were who did not believe, and who it was who would betray him" (John 6:64). Jesus never trusted Judas, who had an important role to fulfill in the events that would lead to the salvation of the world through Jesus Christ.

Let's jump past this day in Holy Week in order to complete the story of Judas. Finding him in the Garden of Gethsemane, Judas betrayed Jesus with a kiss revealing his identity to the soldiers and indicating whom they should arrest (Matt 26:47–50). Later, when Judas realized what he had done and that Jesus had been condemned to death, he was seized with remorse. Judas returned the money, went out and killed himself (Matt 27:1–10).

The response of Judas was undeniably quite extreme, but I wonder how often you and I may have felt like doing the same. Guilt is such a powerful force. When not handled properly, it can certainly result in deep regret. Maybe you feel that no one could forgive you for what you've done. Maybe there's a part of you that doesn't even want to be forgiven. You may have become numb and accustomed to living with guilt. May today be the turning point in your life as you lean in to the graciousness of God's mercy and forgiveness.

Holy Week Today

What are you holding on to of which you need to repent? It may be something small or something that feels insurmountable. Figuratively, take the noose off your neck. With repentance, accept the fact that Jesus willingly hung on a tree and died so that you don't have to. Know that God offers reconciliation to those who approach his throne of grace and mercy. You do not need to carry your guilt any longer. Give it to Jesus.

Holy Wednesday Prayer

adapted from a prayer written by William Barclay

God of love, I remember how Jesus was betrayed, and given up into the hands of wicked men . . .

Lord Jesus, I remember today that it was one of your own familiar friends who betrayed you, and I know that there is nothing that so breaks the heart as the disloyalty of one whom we call friend. Grant that I may not betray you.

Save us:

From the cowardice that would disown you when it is hard to be true to you; from the disloyalty that betrays you in the hour when you need someone to stand by you; from the fickleness that blows hot and cold in its devotion; from the fair–weather friendship that, when things are difficult or dangerous, makes me ashamed to show whose I am and whom I serve.

Let me remember how Jesus suffered death upon the cross . . .

Lord Jesus, help me to remember the lengths to which your love was ready to go; that having loved your own you loved them to the very end; the love than which none can be greater, the love that lays down its life for its friends; that it was while people were yet enemies that you died for them.

Let me remember how Jesus now lives and reigns . . . Help me to remember, that the crucified Lord is the risen Lord; that the cross has become the crown.
So grant unto me, to trust in his love and to live in his presence; that I may share in his glory.

This I ask for your love's sake,
Amen.

Ah, Holy Jesus

Ah, holy Jesus, how hast thou offended,
that we to judge thee have in hate pretended?
By foes derided, by thine own rejected,
O most afflicted!

Who was the guilty? Who brought this upon thee?
Alas, my treason, Jesus, hath undone thee!
'Twas I, Lord Jesus, I it was denied thee;
I crucified thee.

Lo, the Good Shepherd for the sheep is offered;
The slave hath sinned, and the Son hath suffered.
For our atonement, while we nothing heeded,
God interceded.

For me, kind Jesus, was thy incarnation,
thy mortal sorrow, and thy life's oblation;
Thy death of anguish and thy bitter passion,
for my salvation.

Therefore, kind Jesus, since I cannot pay thee,
I do adore thee, and will ever pray thee,
think on thy pity and thy love unswerving,
not my deserving.

Johann Heermann (1630); trans. Robert Bridges (1897)

Maundy Thursday

A New Command

Read: Mark 14:12–16, 22–25

Mandatum novum do vobis ut diligatis invicem sicut dilexi vos

A new commandment I give unto you, that you love one another; as I have loved you.

These words, spoken by Jesus (John 13:34), provides us with the name of this day—Maundy Thursday. Maundy means "mandate" or "command." The Latin *mandatum novum* means new mandate. It was on this day that Jesus gave the command to love one another. This was not a new command for the disciples. They had heard it many times over the course of their lives. After all, the original command is found in the Law of Moses (Lev 19:18). The difference this time was that Jesus modeled how to love others through his act of servanthood by washing the disciples feet. He made the connection of loving others with serving others.

Preparations for the Passover were made Thursday afternoon. Jesus sent two of his disciples to prepare the room where they would observe the Passover. This would not have been an unusual task for the disciples. They expected to observe Passover. In fact, Mark tells us that the disciples asked Jesus, "Where will you have us

STEVEN D. BROOKS

go and prepare for you to eat the Passover?" (Mark 14:12) As Jews, they would have observed Passover every year of their lives. This annual festival was an opportunity for the Jewish community to recall God's deliverance of their people out of Egyptian slavery. This annual feast was incredibly significant to the Jewish people as they remembered their ancestors' deliverance out of Egypt (Mark 14:12–16) and this year wouldn't have been any different. The disciples found an upper room and it is here where several significant events occurred.

Jesus and his disciples celebrated Passover with the traditional liturgy and meal. This time was different though as Jesus instituted what is now known as the Lord's Supper (Matt 26:26–29). Jesus created deeper meaning for the Passover when he took the bread and called it his body and took the cup of wine and called it the new covenant in his blood revealing that the deliverance of the Israelites out of Egypt was a foreshadowing of the deliverance he would offer to the world through his sacrifice on the cross (Matt 26:26–29; Mark 14:22–25; Luke 22:14–20).

During the course of the evening, Jesus got up from the table, took off his outer robe, and tied a towel around himself. He then poured water into a basin and began to wash the disciples' feet and to wipe them with the towel that was tied around him (John 13:1–20). This symbol of servanthood was an example to us all on how to love one another. For it is in connection with washing the disciples' feet that Jesus said, "This is my commandment, that you love one another as I have loved you" (John 15:12).

On this evening, Jesus spent time teaching his disciples. In addition to the "new command" Jesus,

- Told the disciples that he will prepare a place in heaven for all those who believe in him (John 14:3).
- Reiterated that he is the only Way, Truth, and Life and no one is able to have a relationship with the Father except through him (John 14:6).
- Promised the presence of the Holy Spirit to be a Helper (John 14:16).
- Spoke of being the true Vine that his followers must abide in (John 15:1–11).
- Affirmed to the disciples that he has overcome the world (John 16:33).

- Gave an account of his earthly mission to his Father who sent him (John 17:1–5)
- Prayed for his disciples (John 17:6–19)
- Prayed for you and me, concerned for our unity and love (John 17:20–26)

To conclude their time Jesus and his disciples sang a hymn together. From there they crossed the Kidron Valley and entered a garden called Gethsemane to pray. Gethsemane was familiar to them as they often spent time there while visiting Jerusalem (cf. Luke 22:39). Jesus spent time in the garden praying, asking his Father if there was any other way for God's plan to be fulfilled, other than the cross (Mark 14:35–36).

As Jesus prayed in Gethsemane, his disciples slept. It was difficult for them to stay awake. When I think about this situation, it could be easy to judge the disciples for falling asleep at such a critical time. But isn't it hard for us to stay awake sometimes, too? I'm not talking about being awake physically. I'm talking about being awake spiritually. Jesus's prayers were so intense that he needed an angel to come and strengthen him (Luke 22:43). Yet the disciples slept. Even so, the powers of this world continue to battle against Jesus and we his followers, and we too fall into a spiritual sleep. We easily get drawn into the culture and temptations of our world. Our spirits want to do what is right, but our flesh is weak (Mark 14:38). We can easily fail to fulfill our calling as followers of Christ merely by giving into various physical, emotional, and mental needs or desires. We are easily distracted from worship, prayer, solitude, or a kind act by hunger, thirst, exhaustion, sexual desire, feeling too cold or too hot, pain, and even a persistent itch. The flesh shouts loudly when it wants something, and the commotion it makes can easily drown out the desires of the spirit. Even when the spirit is willing to do whatever God asks, the flesh remains weak. The answer? Jesus tells his disciples to watch and pray. Jesus had to awaken his disciples and lovingly rebuke them and may he do the same for us.

Holy Week Today

If you are currently struggling and need an encouraging word, be assured that all believers know the struggle of Jesus's statement "the spirit indeed is willing, but the flesh is weak" (Matt 26:41). But when we obey Jesus by watching and praying—when we remain spiritually alert and appeal to God for help—we can find strength in the time of need (see Ps 46:1; Heb 4:16). And when we fail, "we have an advocate with the Father—Jesus Christ, the Righteous One. He is the atoning sacrifice for our sins, and not only for ours but also for the sins of the whole world" (1 John 2:1–2).

While we keep watch awaiting the return of Christ the King, may we live according to Jesus's command to love one another. Consider the ways you can show God's love to those you come into contact with today. Showing kindness is one of the simplest but most profound ways to show God's love. Other ways include being a good listener, being generous with your time and talents, offering words of encouragement to others who need it, and genuinely praying for their needs or thanking God for them. How can you show God's love to someone today?

Maundy Thursday Prayer

Oh Lord, may I be ever watchful.

May I keep my eyes focused on you, Jesus.

Help me see opportunities to show love to others, through acts of kindness, mercy, and compassion.

When you return, may you find me "awake" fulfilling your calling upon my life.

May I live my life in such a way that at the end of my time, may I hear,

"Well done!"

Amen.

I Love the Lord

I love the Lord; he heard my cries
and pitied every groan:
Long as I live, when troubles rise,
I'll hasten to his throne.

I love the Lord; he bowed his ear,
and chased my griefs away;
O let my heart no more despair,
while I have breath to pray!

My flesh declined, my spirits fell,
and I drew near the dead,
while inward pangs, and fears of hell,
perplexed my wakeful head.

'My God,' I cried, 'thy servant save,
thou ever good and just;
Thy power can rescue from the grave,
thy power is all my trust.'

The Lord beheld me sore distress,
he bid my pains remove:
Return, my soul, to God, thy rest,
for thou hast known his love.

My God hath saved my soul from death,
and dried my falling tears;
Now to his praise I'll spend my breath,
and my remaining years.

Isaac Watts (1719)

Good Friday

What's So Good About Good Friday?

Read: John 19:16b–30

There is nothing about the events of this day that can be considered good.

Garden. Prayer. Distress. Troubled. Disciples. Sleeping. Awake! Judas. Betrayal. Kiss. Soldiers. Chief Priests. Pharisees. Lanterns. Torches. Weapons. Overwhelmed. Sword. Ear. Healing. Arrest. High Priest. Annas. Courtyard. Peter. Deny. Deny. Deny. Rooster. Mocking. Beating. Caiaphas. Pilate. Not guilty. Herod. Contempt. Pilate. Not guilty. Barabbas. Murderer. Released. Pilate. Basin. Hands washed. Jesus. Flogged. Scourged. Crown of thorns. Scarlet robe. Beating. Spitting. Beating. Mocking. Beating. Crucify! Crucify! Cross. Simon of Cyrene. Golgotha. Place of the Skull. Two criminals. Today. Paradise. Sign. Jesus. Nazareth. King. Jews. Forgive them. Garments. Lots. Gambling. Mary. Son. John. Mother. Thirst. Sponge. Sour wine. Darkness. Forsaken. Finished. Death. Curtain. Torn. Earthquake. Tombs. Spear. Side. Blood. Water. Burial. Garden.

This "good" day is filled with horrendous events that are anything but good. We may be told this day is called good because of what was accomplished for believers by Jesus on the cross. Though this is true, the more accurate meaning of the day's name comes from the meaning of the Old English word "good," which means "holy" or "righteous." This day is a holy day. Friday of Holy Week.

Observing Good Friday dates back to the fourth century as seen in the writings of Egeria, one of the earliest documented Christian pilgrims, who visited the most important destinations in the eastern Mediterranean between 381 and 384 AD. She wrote an account of her travels and experiences, which are among the earliest descriptions of pilgrimage travel to the Holy Land and beyond.

Egeria wrote that Friday was the most solemn day of the "Great Week" in Jerusalem and the three–hour service that began at noon was incredibly meaningful to her. From the sixth to the ninth hour (12:00 P.M.–3:00 P.M.), passages from Scripture were continuously read and hymns were sung. And so during these three hours all the people were taught that nothing happened which was not prophesied, and that nothing was prophesied which was not completely fulfilled. Egeria comments that every one, young and old, was moved to tears with the realization that the Lord suffered for them.

In addition to ancient writings, we also have foreshadowing (or prophecy) of Jesus's death in the Old Testament—including the book of Isaiah and the Psalms. A comparison of the Gospel accounts of the crucifixion with details from Psalm 22 and Isaiah 53 compliments our understanding of its importance:

CRUCIFIXION DETAIL	GOSPEL	PSALM	ISAIAH
"My God, my God, why have you forsaken me?"	Matt 26:46	Ps 22:1	
They derided him, wagging their heads	Matt 27:39	Ps 22:7	Is 53:3
They mocked him	Matt 27:29, 41	Ps 22:7	
"He trusts in God. Let God rescue him now"	Matt 27:43	Ps 22:8	
They surrounded him	Mark 15:16–20	Ps 22:12–13	
They pierced him	John 19:34	Ps 22:16	Is 53:5
They took his clothes and divided them	John 20:23–24	Ps 22:18	
Jesus breathed his last	Mark 15:37	Ps 22:15	Is 53:9

The first Christians were entirely distraught by the tragic death of Jesus. They felt lost and confused. They had heard the prophecies of Isaiah and had sung the songs of the psalmists which told of a servant who was chosen and sent to bring hope to the people. This hope, however, was brought in a rather unconventional way that many missed or misunderstood. It is this hope that is the principal foundation of this dreadful day in Holy Week.

Amidst the tragedy of the events of this day we

perceive that Good Friday is fundamentally a story of grace and of God's love for us. The Father sent his Son into our world. The Son showed us perfect love—a love so great that he freely paid the price for our sins and the sins of the whole world. The gift of that grace and love is offered to all. As John 3:16 poignantly reminds us:

> For God so loved the world, that he gave
> his only Son, that whoever believes in him
> should not perish but have eternal life.

This excerpt of a conversation between Jesus and Nicodemus is the best known declaration of God's love. God's love is indestructible as neither man's fall in the Garden nor the many violations in the course of human history since have caused his love for humankind to diminish. God loves the world, as hostile as it often is to him, continually and unwaveringly.

God's great love displayed in offering his Son as the payment for the sin of the world is the catalyst of our fellowship with God.

> For God did not send his Son into the
> world to condemn the world, but in order

that the world might be saved through
him. (John 3:17)

Those who put their faith and trust in Jesus as Lord gain
eternal life because of Christ's sacrifice.

Jesus Christ is the sacrifice given once for all (Heb
7:27; 10:10). The Paschal Lamb (1 Cor 5:6–8), who
was slain to take away the sins of the world (John 1:29;
Eph 1:5–7; Heb 9:12–14). Our sins were eliminated by
the sacrifice of our Savior, covered by the blood of the
Lamb. And that is definitely good!

Holy Week Today

Did you know that Joseph of Arimathea had been a
secret follower of Christ because he feared the Jews
(John 19:38)? The crucifixion of Jesus, however, was
a turning point for Joseph. After the crucifixion, he
went to Pilate and boldly asked for Jesus's body. Joseph
risked his reputation among the religious leaders to give
his Lord a proper burial. When Joseph laid Jesus's body
in his own tomb, he showed both great love and great
courage.

Is fear keeping you a secret follower of Jesus? Would

standing up for your faith in Christ threaten your reputation? If so, remember Joseph of Arimathea. Don't let fear keep you from being a bold follower of Jesus. Take up your cross and follow him courageously today assured that God will secure you in his grasp.

Good Friday Prayer

Father, thank you for sending your one and only Son. Thank you that we can have great hope, for death has lost its sting. We praise you for you are making all things new.

Jesus, thank you for your ultimate sacrifice. We remember today, the pain and suffering of the cross, and all that you were willing to endure, so we could be set free. You paid the price, such a great sacrifice, to offer us the gift of eternal life.

Spirit of God, help us never to take for granted the gift of love on our behalf. Help us to be reminded of the cost of it all and encourage us to keep our eyes focused on Jesus Christ, the only name that saves.

May we live our lives in ways that are worthy of Jesus's sacrifice.

Amen.

Go to Dark Gethsemane

Go to dark Gethsemane,
ye that feel the tempter's power;
Your Redeemer's conflict see,
watch with him one bitter hour;
Turn not from his griefs away;
Learn of Jesus Christ to pray.

Follow to the judgment hall;
View the Lord of life arraigned;
O the wormwood and gall!
O the pangs his souls sustained!
Shun not suffering, shame, or loss;
Learn of him to bear the cross.

Calvary's mournful mountain climb;
There, adoring at his feet,
mark the miracle of time,
God's own sacrifice complete;
"It is finished!" hear him cry;
Learn of Jesus Christ to die.

James Montgomery (1825)

7

Holy Saturday

Worship in the Waiting

Read: John 19:38–42

Yesterday was Good Friday, the starkest and most sorrowful day of the Christian year, and tomorrow will be Easter Sunday, the most joyful and celebratory. Today, Holy Saturday, is that in–between day, the "already but not yet," where Christ lay in the tomb. This is a day when the cross seems all too real and the resurrection is only a rumor of things yet to be.

Not much is said in Scripture regarding the day after Jesus's death. Matthew is the only one of the four Gospels who tells us something about this day.

> The next day, the one after Preparation Day, the chief priests and the Pharisees went to Pilate. "Sir," they said, "we remember that while he was still alive that deceiver said, 'After three days I will rise again.' So give the order for the tomb to be made secure until the third day. Otherwise, his disciples may come and steal the body and tell the people that he has been raised from the dead. This last deception will be worse than the first." "Take a guard,"

Pilate answered. "Go, make the tomb as secure as you know how." So they went and made the tomb secure by putting a seal on the stone and posting the guard. (Matt 27:62–66)

There are many theological speculations concerning what Jesus did on this day. Mainly because Scripture does not tell us. Now, you may be asking, what do you mean, "What Jesus did on this day"? Wasn't he dead? Well yes . . . and no.

If you are a Christian, you must become accustomed to paradox. Followers of Christ must trust in the infallibility of Scripture believing the Bible is one hundred percent trustworthy and without error. However, God's Word contains many paradoxes—statements that appear contradictory on the surface when paired next to one another. Understood in context though, such statements complement one another to reveal a more full picture of truth.

For instance, throughout Scripture, we are told not to fear (Is 41:10) and to fear the Lord (Ps 33:8). We are told to be bold (Josh 1:9) and to be humble (James 4:10). We are told not to judge (Matt 7:1) and to judge according to righteous judgement (John 7:24). The last will be first and the first will be last (Matt 20:16). When we are weak, then we are strong (2 Cor 12:10). And then the ultimate paradox—Jesus himself. Jesus was one hundred percent God and one hundred percent man.

On this day the one hundred percent God–man was dead, but the one hundred percent God–divine was very much still alive. And I do not believe that Jesus, the divine, just sat in the tomb waiting for Sunday.

Through the centuries, many questions have arisen about what Jesus experienced on this day. Did he sleep, as if in a great Sabbath rest? Was he in "paradise" (Luke 23:43), a blissful state considered by some in Jesus's day to be a part of Sheol, known also as Abraham's bosom (Luke 19:22)? Was he proclaiming his victory to the spirits of the dead and beings held "below"? These are great questions and seeking answers can lead to healthy considerations of the person and work of Jesus, but also into possible controversy, as even biblical scholars can't agree on the events of this day. Yet we do not need to have our questions resolved to experience the biblical value of Holy Saturday.

Here is what we do know about this day:

- Jesus, the man, was dead and his body lay in the grave.

- His disciples were hiding behind locked doors in fear for their lives. This day was the Sabbath, a day of worship. And not just any Sabbath, but the Sabbath of Passover, a "special Sabbath." The disciples should have been worshiping in the temple rejoicing in the deliverance of the people of God. And yet they were hiding away, full of grief, trembling in fear instead of participating in joyful worship.

- The women, identified as Mary Magdalene, Mary the mother of James, and Salome (Mark 16:1), likely with others as well, were waiting for Sunday so they could take spices and ointments needed to prepare Jesus's body. John tells us that Nicodemus took a mixture of myrrh and aloes to the tomb with Jesus's body, as well as linen cloths and spices, according to the Jewish burial custom. So why does Mark tell us the women went to the tomb on Sunday morning with spices to anoint Jesus? Did the women not know that Nicodemus already prepared Jesus's body? Or, did Nicodemus not actually prepare Jesus's body properly, simply choosing to allow the women the privilege of doing so on Sunday. If Nicodemus did prepare Jesus's body, did the women feel more was required or did they simply want to participate in the custom as well? Scripture does not tell us. What Scripture does tell us is that neither Nicodemus nor the women needed to prepare Jesus's body for burial because the preparation had already taken place two days beforehand. Mark tells us that a woman in Bethany anointed Jesus with oil from an alabaster jar (Mark 14:3–9). In response, Jesus told his disciples that "she has anointed my body beforehand for burial" (Mark 14:8). God, in his ultimate plan, knowing there would not be time to properly prepare Jesus's body for burial on Friday, and that he would be risen by the time the women arrived on Sunday, had this woman do so days before. What an amazing God!

- Guards, per the Matthew passage above, were placed at the entrance of the tomb to deter Jesus's disciples from stealing his body and claiming he rose from the dead.

One temptation on this day is to jump right to Easter and the resurrection—to celebrate our risen Savior. But this day before Easter Sunday is critically important to our spiritual growth. It is a day of waiting. As Christians, we need to learn better how to wait. Although there are times it may seem as though God is silent, he is actively at work behind the scenes. Don't you think Jesus could have been raised from the dead on Saturday; or within hours after his crucifixion? Yes, of course he could have. But God waited. And he made the disciples wait. And sometimes he makes us wait. Oftentimes the waiting period is a time to see if we truly trust in the sovereignty of God.

This day is also a day of grieving. Early Christians, and others today, call this day the "Paschal Vigil." A vigil is a time to mourn the loss of a loved one as family and friends gather either in the home of the deceased, in the funeral home, or in the church to pray and remember the departed. Some may call this a viewing. A viewing, just like a vigil, allows mourners the opportunity to share their grief, support one another, and say goodbye on a personal level. This is also considered an important event for showing your respects to the family. On Holy

Saturday we have an opportunity to allow ourselves to grieve the death of Jesus, but to do so with hope and anticipation of what is to come.

Holy Saturday often gets skipped over. Do not pass this day by. It is an important day in Holy Week. It is important for the spiritual formation of our inner beings. We get caught up in anticipating the celebration of Easter the next day and forget that Saturday is a significant part of the story too. While we know the end of the story and live in the hope of the resurrection, feeling the weight of Jesus's death before we celebrate his resurrection is valuable for understanding the depth of what Christ did for us through his sacrifice. Let's not rush through this day. Jesus was crucified. His body laid in a tomb. The Lamb slain. Hope seemed to be lost. But we remember something Jesus said about rising from the dead in three days . . . and so we wait.

Holy Week Today

This may be the most difficult day of Holy Week because we don't like to wait. But don't skip over this day. Instead, allow yourself to feel the weight of Jesus's death. Remember that he loved you so much that he willingly died for you. Don't rush to the celebration. Sit. Breathe. Be Still. Reflect.

Today, as you reflect upon Jesus's sacrifice, my prayer is that Christ may dwell in your heart through faith and that you will be rooted and grounded in the love of Christ. May you have the "strength to comprehend with all the saints what is the breadth and length and height and depth, and to know the love of Christ that surpasses knowledge, that you may be filled with all the fullness of God" (Eph 3:18–19).

Holy Saturday Prayer

based on Psalm 62:5–12

Father, my salvation and honor come from you alone.
For you are my refuge, and my Rock.
*I wait quietly before you God, for my hope is in you, my Rock
and my Salvation.*

Lord I am yours. Help me to trust you at all times. I
desire to pour out my heart to you, for you are my refuge.
*I wait quietly before you God, for my hope is in you, my Rock
and my Salvation.*

From the greatest to the lowliest—all are nothing in
your sight. If you weigh them on the scales, they are
lighter than a puff of air.
*I wait quietly before you God, for my hope is in you, my Rock
and my Salvation.*

God you have spoken plainly—I have heard it many
times. Power, O God, belongs to you; unfailing love, O
Lord, is yours.
*I wait quietly before you God, for my hope is in you, my Rock
and my Salvation.*

In the Cross of Christ I Glory

In the cross of Christ I glory,
towering o'er the wrecks of time;
All the light of sacred story
gathers round its head sublime.

When the woes of life o'ertake me,
hopes deceive, and fears annoy,
never shall the cross forsake me.
Lo! it glows with peace and joy.

When the sun of bliss is beaming
light and love upon my way,
from the cross the radiance streaming
adds more luster to the day.

Bane and blessing, pain and pleasure,
by the cross are sanctified;
Peace is there that knows no measure,
joys that through all time abide.

In the cross of Christ I glory,
towering o'er the wrecks of time;
All the light of sacred story
gathers round its head sublime.

John Bowring (1825)

Easter Sunday

He Is Risen Indeed!

Read: Matthew 28:1–7

Easter Sunday begins a new season of the Christian Year and is not part of Holy Week, but I just couldn't stop my reflections on Saturday with Jesus lying in the tomb.

CHRIST IS RISEN!

Today is the greatest day in history—the resurrection of Jesus Christ! This day is critically important not only for the church, but for the entire world. It is the most pivotal event in human history. For centuries this day has also been called "The Great Day."

The resurrection of Jesus is foundational to the Christian faith and is so important that the Apostle Paul writes:

> If Christ has not been raised, your faith is futile and you are still in your sins. (1 Cor 15:17)

And later he says:

> If in Christ we have hope in this life only, we are of all people most to be pitied. (1 Cor 15:19)

Paul knew of the importance of the resurrection and he was persistent in preaching Christ and his resurrection.

HE IS RISEN INDEED!

The death and resurrection of Jesus are the central events of the Christian faith. The miraculous resurrection gave assurance to Jesus's disciples, and to Christians of all times, that Jesus really is the Son of God. It verified the truth of the whole testimony of Jesus and gave authority to his teachings.

The first generation of Jesus's followers believed he had risen, and were convinced that everything had changed as a result. Over five hundred witnesses testified to the accuracy of Jesus's resurrection, many of whom gave up their own lives because of their testimony and faith. The apostles were willing to die for this truth. Furthermore, Jesus's resurrection was so important for followers of Christ that they made this day, Sunday, a new day of meeting to commemorate his resurrection.

ALLELUIA! ALLELUIA!

Christ's resurrection gives us assurance that we too will be raised from the dead. Just as Adam brought sin and death into the world, Jesus Christ brings life through the promised hope of resurrection. All those who put their faith and trust in Jesus don't just look forward to heaven, but a bodily resurrection as well (see 1 Cor 15:20–28). Easter is the promise that an empty tomb means that those who have died in Christ, having placed their hope and trust in the living Savior, will be justified and raised from the dead.

And yet resurrection is not only a future event for believers because those who believe in Christ have already been raised to life with him. Paul writes:

> If then you have been raised with Christ, seek the things that are above, where Christ is, seated at the right hand of God. (Col 3:1)

Christians are people who have already been raised with Christ. Therefore it is accurate to say that the resurrection is an already but not–yet reality for the Christian. Jesus's resurrection means that those who have faith in him have been raised from the dead because they are in Christ, and yet they still await the full experience of the resurrection to come (Rom 8:22–23).

In addition to calling Easter Sunday, "The Great Sunday," the church has called every Sunday of the year a "little resurrection day." This is a good reminder that we should not cease to celebrate our risen Lord with only one Sunday in the year. Every time we gather together to worship, let us celebrate the fact that Jesus Christ has risen, conquering death and the grave, and has offered us new life in him. We join with the Apostle Paul in declaring:

> Death is swallowed up in victory. O death, where is your victory? O death, where is your sting? The sting of death is sin, and the power of sin is the law. But thanks be to God, who gives us victory through the Lord Jesus Christ." (1 Cor 15:54–57)

ALLELUIA! ALLELUIA!

Holy Week Today

What does Easter mean to you?

As we celebrate Easter we are celebrating God's great love for us, a love strong enough to defeat death itself. Jesus is alive and living within his people. Do you know the joy of living according to Jesus's life instead of your own?

Today, commit to living your life in ways that act justly in response to your surrounding circumstances, show mercy to those around you, as you walk humbly with God (Micah 6:8).

Easter Sunday Prayer

Father, because of Easter we can declare:

Where, O death, is your victory?

Where, O death, is your sting?

Thanks be to God who gives us victory over death!

We rejoice in Christ our Savior as life bursts from death.

We hold our heads high because Christ is risen!

Jesus Christ is alive forevermore!

Alleluia!

Amen.

Christ the Lord Is Risen Today

Christ the Lord is risen today, alleluia!
Earth and heaven in chorus say, alleluia!
Raise your joys and triumphs high, alleluia!
Sing, ye heavens, and earth reply, alleluia!

Love's redeeming work is done, alleluia!
Fought the fight, the battle won, alleluia!
Death in vain forbids him rise, alleluia!
Christ has opened paradise, alleluia!

Lives again our glorious King, alleluia!
Where, O death, is now thy sting? alleluia!
Once he died our souls to save, alleluia!
Where's thy victory, boasting grave? alleluia!

Soar we now where Christ has led, alleluia!
Following our exalted head, alleluia!
Made like him, like him we rise, alleluia!
Ours the cross, the grave, the skies, alleluia!

Hail the Lord of earth and heaven, alleluia!
Praise to thee by both be given, alleluia!
Thee we greet triumphant now, alleluia!
Hail the resurrection, thou, alleluia!

King of glory, soul of bliss, alleluia!
Everlasting life is this, alleluia!
Thee to know, thy power to prove, alleluia!
Thus to sing, and thus to love, alleluia!

Charles Wesley (1739)

Conclusion

To walk with Jesus on his journey through Holy Week provides spiritual nourishment for our souls. It draws us toward a deeper relationship with Christ, our suffering Savior, and ushers us to new life through his resurrection. The events of this week, the end of Jesus's three years of earthly ministry, fulfilled the Father's ultimate plan for the beginning of the process of renewal for all of creation. And yet the process is not complete. We continue to wait for Christ to come again in all his glory to usher in a new creation . . . a re–creation. In the meantime, we will worship in remembrance with hope until he returns. Maranatha— come, Lord Jesus.

Holy Week Today

At the beginning of this week, I encouraged you to select something that you would abstain from (fasting, solitude, etc.) and choose a spiritual habit to engage in that will encourage more of Jesus to fill its place (Bible reading, prayer, etc.). I mentioned that I firmly believed that doing so would make a significant impact upon your spiritual life. So how did it go? I pray the experience was a positive one that encourages you to practice abstaining as well as engaging spiritual habits on a regular basis. If not throughout the entire year, than definitely during the season of Lent as you prepare for the worship and celebration of Christ's resurrection at Easter.

Bonus Reflection

Pour My Love On You

Read: Mark 14:3–9

Two days before Passover (Mark 14:1), Jesus was in Bethany (approximately 2 miles outside of Jerusalem; John 11:18) with his disciples visiting Simon the leper. During the visit an incredible moment of worship occurs during the meal at Simon's home.

There are a few points to consider within this story. First, we are not told the purpose of this gathering, but it may have been a special feast rather than a regular meal because Jesus was reclining at the table. This position was the common practice for banquets, rather than an everyday meal.

In addition, the amount of ointment used for the anointing was said to be worth three hundred denarii, which was a rather large quantity and cost the equivalent of approximately one year's wages (a denarius was a day's wage for a laborer). This was an incredible act of sacrifice as she poured out her love upon Jesus. Even if the meal was not part of a special occasion, this woman transformed it into one by her level of sacrifice and act of worship.

Although these are important points to consider, it is Jesus's response to the disciples that captures my attention. His response advises us that our first and foremost responsibility is to worship Jesus. It is important to note that Jesus is not discouraging helping the poor. We know from Jesus's life and ministry that caring for the least of these is a very important function of Christ followers. The "concern" of the disciples is evident in pointing out that the oil could have been sold and the money given to the poor (remember, it was one year's worth of wages). That amount of money could provide a lot of food and clothing. It could help with rent. This money could have been put in a benevolence fund. The ministry of care, however, should never come before our worship of the One who calls us to that ministry in the first place. Here, in this moment, Jesus makes the point that now is the time to worship.

Furthermore, Jesus clarifies that this act of worship is preparing him for his burial. This seems like such an interesting statement, doesn't it? As mentioned in our Saturday reflection, this special event goes beyond the worship–filled room of Simon the leper's house. This is a critical moment within God's plan to prepare Jesus's body for his burial. There would be no time to do so on Friday after his crucifixion. Many biblical scholars believe that the timeframe for Jesus's crucifixion was between nine o'clock in the morning until three o'clock in the afternoon. By the time Joseph of Arimathea received permission from Pilate to bury Jesus in his own grave (John 19:38), returned to Golgotha, transported Jesus's body to the grave, and moved the extremely heavy stone to seal the tomb (this would have been a very large, heavy stone that would have required multiple people to move), it would have been near sunset, or for the Jewish community, the next day (since the new day begins at sundown). So what day would this be? This new day was the Sabbath (Saturday). Since no work is permitted on the Sabbath, Jesus's burial needed to be completed before sundown on Friday. They were working against the clock—or should I say, the sun. Therefore, there was no time to properly prepare Jesus's body for burial. Scripture informs us, however, that his body did not need to be prepared because the preparation had already been done days before with his anointing in Simon's home.

Was this simply an act of worship for this woman or did she understand the greater plan of God in all this? I'm not sure it really matters. The fact is that our primary responsibility is to worship Jesus. And our worship will be received and have an impact beyond what we could ever imagine.

Holy Week Today

Today, spend time pouring out your love on Jesus. Just as the woman's worship affected those present in the room, allow your worship to overflow so that those around you will sense your love for God and your love for them.

Prayer

Lord, today I bring my alabaster jar of worship to you. I don't want to offer that which costs me nothing, for you deserve more than I could ever give. So today I bring those things which are precious to me. I pour them out to you Jesus, freely and generously. They may be hard to let go of, but I know it is those things which are exactly what you appreciate receiving from me. Jesus, may my actions be an authentic offering of worship to you and an encouragement to others to do the same.

I pray this in the precious name of Jesus,

Amen.

My Song Is Love Unknown

My song is love unknown,
my Savior's love to me,
love to the loveless shown,
that they might lovely be.
O who am I, that for my sake
my Lord should take frail flesh and die?

He came from his blest throne,
salvation to bestow;
But men cared not, and none
the longed–for Christ would know.
But oh, my Friend, my Friend indeed,
who at my need his life did spend!

Sometimes they strew his way,
and his sweet praises sing;
Resounding all the day
hosannas to their King.
Then "Crucify!" is all their breath,
and for his death they thirst and cry.

Why, what hath my Lord done?
What makes this rage and spite?
He made the lame to run,

he gave the blind their sight.
Sweet injuries! Yet all his deeds
their hatred feeds; they 'gainst him rise.

They rise, and needs will have
my dear Lord sent away;
A murderer they save,
the Prince of Life they slay.
Yet willing he to suff'ring goes,
that he his foes from thence might free.

In life, no house, no home
my Lord on earth might have;
In death, no friendly tomb
but what a stranger gave.
What may I say? Heav'n was his home,
but mine the tomb wherein he lay.

Here might I stay and sing,
no story so divine;
Never was love, dear King,
never was grief like thine.
This is my Friend, in whose sweet praise
I all my days could gladly spend.

Samuel Crossman (1664)

Benediction

From Palm Sunday to Holy Saturday,
may God in his infinite mercy
grant you a journey of renewal and hope;
A time of prayer and reflection;
And joyful anticipation of our Lord's resurrection.

May you live for the honor and glory of Jesus's name
and serve in remembrance of Christ's love.
We pray in the name of the Father,
of the Son, and of the Holy Spirit.

Amen.